THRILLING SCIENCE AND TECHNOLOGY JOBS

# MODERN INVENTORS

Ruth Owen and John Willis

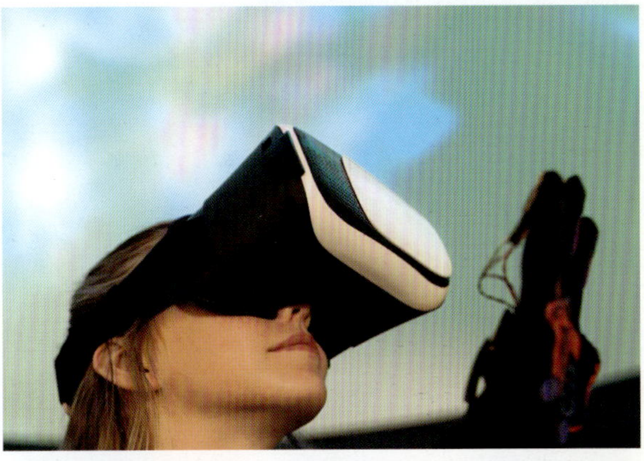

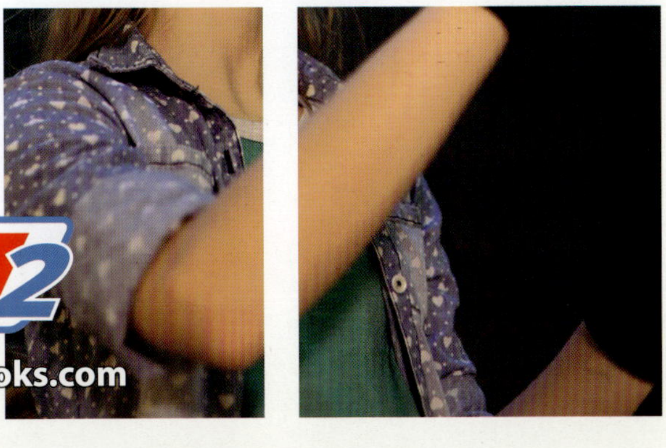

AV2
www.av2books.com

# Step 1
Go to **www.av2books.com**

# Step 2
Enter this unique code

**YUZVF7SHB**

# Step 3
Explore your interactive eBook!

**AV2 is optimized for use on any device**

# Your interactive eBook comes with...

**Contents**
Browse a live contents page to easily navigate through resources

**Audio**
Listen to sections of the book read aloud

**Videos**
Watch informative video clips

**Weblinks**
Gain additional information for research

**Try This!**
Complete activities and hands-on experiments

**Key Words**
Study vocabulary, and complete a matching word activity

**Quizzes**
Test your knowledge

**Slideshows**
View images and captions

## ... and much, much more!

THRILLING SCIENCE AND TECHNOLOGY JOBS

# MODERN INVENTORS

## Contents

# Inventing Our World

There is one thing that humans are very, very good at—inventing!

Almost everything around you was once someone's invention. Without an ancient inventor who discovered that crushed plant fibers could be mixed with water, squeezed flat, and dried, we would not have paper. Without Johannes Gutenberg, who invented the printing press in the 1440s, paper would not be printed and turned into books.

From the first stone tools, invented by our early ancestors, to smartphones and robots, people have been dreaming, designing, making, and using inventions for millions of years.

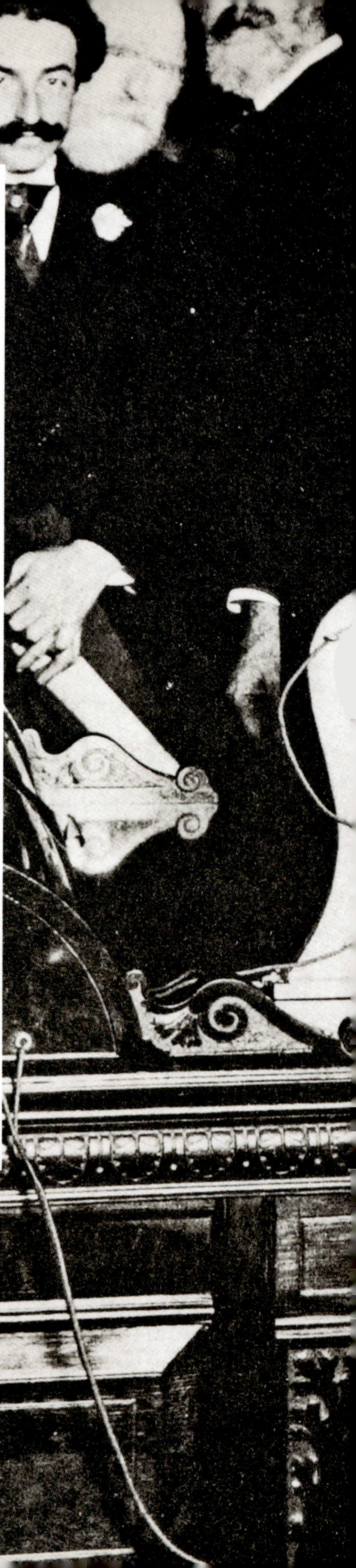

In the late 1870s, Scottish inventor Alexander Graham Bell produced the first telephone that could transmit sounds. He and his assistant, Thomas Watson, made the world's first telephone call.

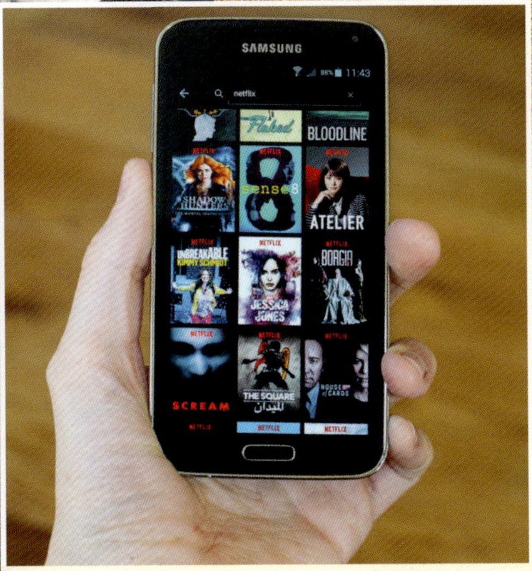


Today's inventors have designed smartphones that can be used for speaking, texting, going online, watching movies, and more.

The **first inventions**, such as stone hand axes, can be dated back **one million years**.

The **Gregorian calendar** system used now was invented in **1582** by Pope Gregory XIII.

Screws, nails, and bolts were invented sometime around **400 BC**. It would be difficult to build furniture, houses, or bridges without these.

# An Inventor's World

Is an inventor a scientist? An **engineer**? A **designer**? Usually, an inventor is all three of these things and more.

An inventor may be the first person to create an entirely new object or a new way of doing something. Sometimes, however, inventors create new and improved versions of things that already exist.

Inventors look at the world and see problems that need to be fixed. Then they work on invention ideas that could solve the problem.

Inventors might use simple equipment such as a notebook and pencil. They may also work with computers, electronics equipment, wood or metalworking tools, or 3D printers.

Shaking thick ketchup from the bottom of a glass bottle was always difficult. The solution to the problem was to invent an upside-down, squeezable plastic bottle.

## INVENTIVE

Inventors might do their work in **laboratories**, workshops, or offices. They may work alone, developing their own ideas, or be employed by big companies as part of a team in the research and development (R&D) department.

# An Invention Comes to Life

It is not enough to just have an exciting idea. Inventors must make the idea come to life. They need to go through the steps of researching, designing, building, and testing a **prototype**.

Once an inventor has an idea, he or she must do research. Who will use the invention? What is the most **cost-effective** way to produce it? Are there older versions of the invention out there already? How will the inventor's new version be better?

Next, the inventor gets to work on designs. He or she might sketch out designs on paper, or create them using a computer program. What materials will be used to make the invention? How will it work?

Once the design is ready, an inventor builds a prototype, or test version, of the invention. The prototype may just be made from scraps of wood and metal. The prototype is tested and the results analyzed. The inventor should show the prototype to as many people as possible to get **feedback**.

Often the design does not work, but this is not a bad thing. When a design fails, it allows an inventor to redesign and improve the idea. Sometimes a mistake may lead to the accidental discovery of something exciting!

# Memorials to Famous Inventors

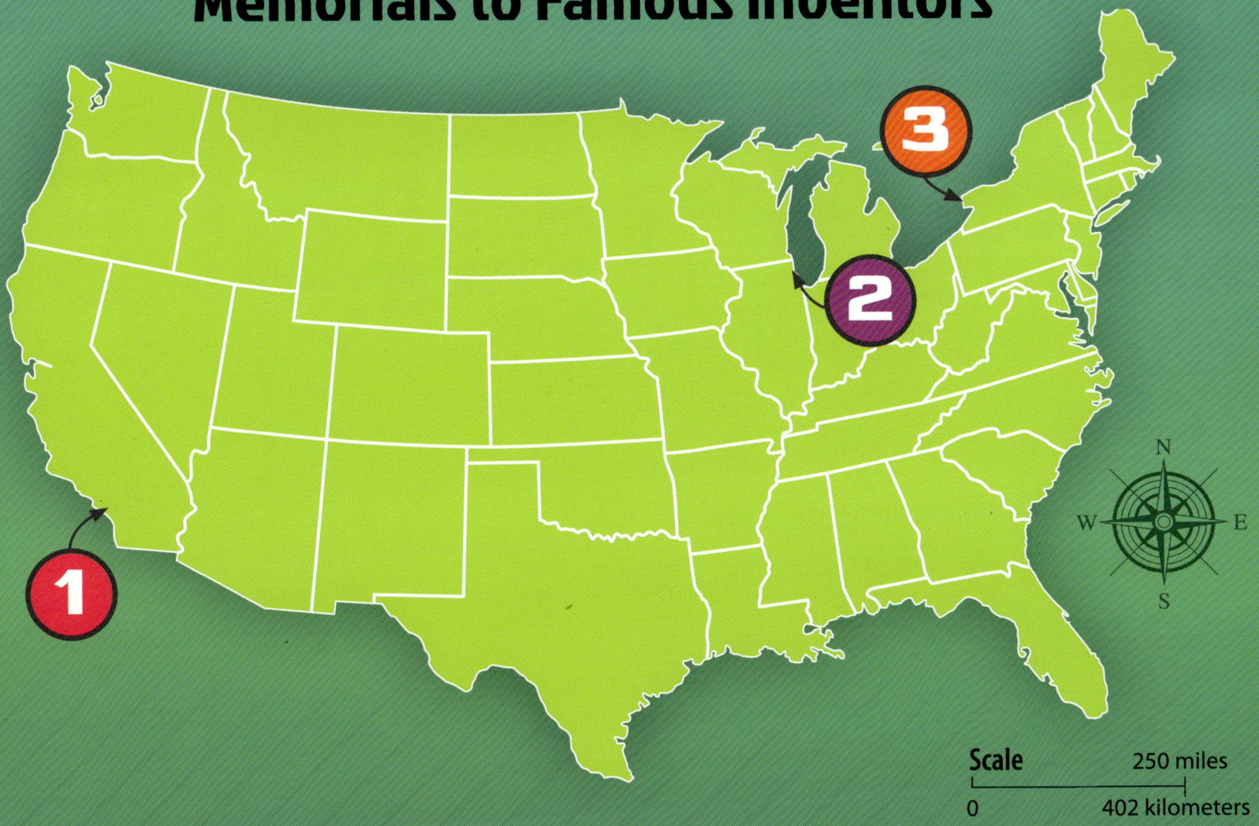

**Steve Jobs Building, Burbank, California**

Steve Jobs was well known as the head of Apple. Before that, he was CEO and owner of Pixar. After his death in 2011, Pixar renamed their main building after him.

**Sarah E. Goode STEM Academy, Chicago, Illinois**

In 1885, Sarah E. Goode became the first African American woman to receive a patent for an invention. She invented a cabinet that could transform into a bed. The academy that was named after her encourages young people to enter **STEM**-related fields.

**Nikola Tesla Statue, Niagara Falls, New York**

Nikola Tesla was an inventor in the late 1800s and early 1900s. His ideas greatly influenced how electricity is used today. His statue in Niagara Falls is located near two hydroelectric power plants that his work helped create.

# Ocean Cleanup: The Problem

Some inventors design a useful gadget or a fun toy. Others, such as Dutch inventor Boyan Slat, take on larger projects. Boyan is tackling one of the biggest environmental problems our planet faces—ocean pollution!

Every year, up to 13 million tons (11.8 million metric tons) of plastic trash enters the oceans. Bottles and food packages discarded on beaches get washed out to sea. Rivers carry plastic bags and other garbage into the ocean. Shipping containers filled with plastic pellets, ready to be made into products in factories, are sometimes washed overboard from ships during storms.

Ocean animals, such as fish, seabirds, and turtles, are killed when they eat plastic waste, thinking it is food. As bottles and other plastic items break up, they release harmful chemicals into the water.

Boyan was still in high school when he began work on his plans to clean up the ocean.

## INVENTIVE

Plastic trash does not decompose, or rot. It simply breaks up into smaller and smaller pieces. These tiny particles, known as microplastics, may remain floating in the ocean forever.

# Ocean Cleanup: The Research

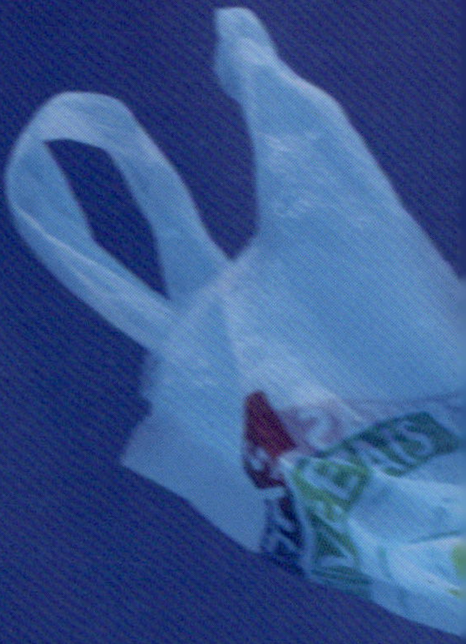

While scuba diving in Greece in 2011, Boyan Slat saw more plastic bags in the ocean than fish and other animals. He realized he wanted to do something to help and got to work researching the issue as a school project. How much plastic is in the ocean? Does it only float at the surface or deeper down, too?

Boyan learned that vast areas of circling water, called **gyres**, form in the Earth's oceans. As ocean **currents** flow into a gyre, the plastic goes, too.

Boyan had an idea. Could a system be devised to capture the plastic waste within the garbage patches?

Garbage patches can become very large over time. The biggest is the Great Pacific Garbage Patch.

Turtles accidentally eat plastic bags because they think they are jellyfish.

## INVENTIVE

On research expeditions in Greece, Boyan trawled the surface of the ocean using a net system called a manta trawl. He could then analyze how much plastic was captured in the net and what size the pieces of plastic were.

# Ocean Cleanup: The Idea

Boyan wanted to devise a system that would allow the ocean to help clean itself! Boyan's original invention was called the Ocean Cleanup Array. A V-shaped floating barrier would be positioned in a gyre. Then, the ocean's currents would slowly funnel, or carry, the plastic waste in the V to an extraction platform. The plastic would be removed from the water and stored on the platform. Then a boat would visit the array to collect the plastic and carry it back to land.

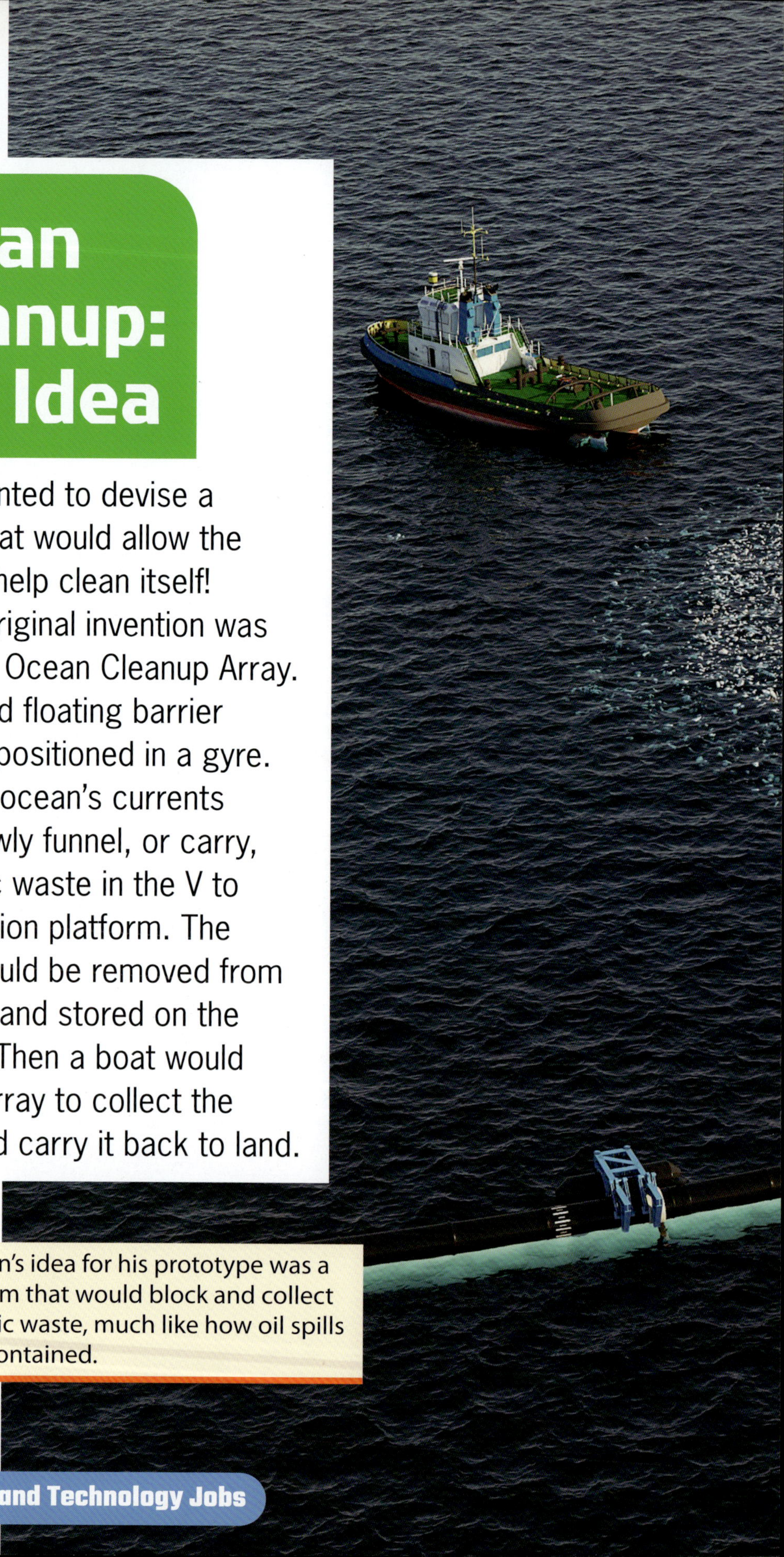

Boyan's idea for his prototype was a system that would block and collect plastic waste, much like how oil spills are contained.

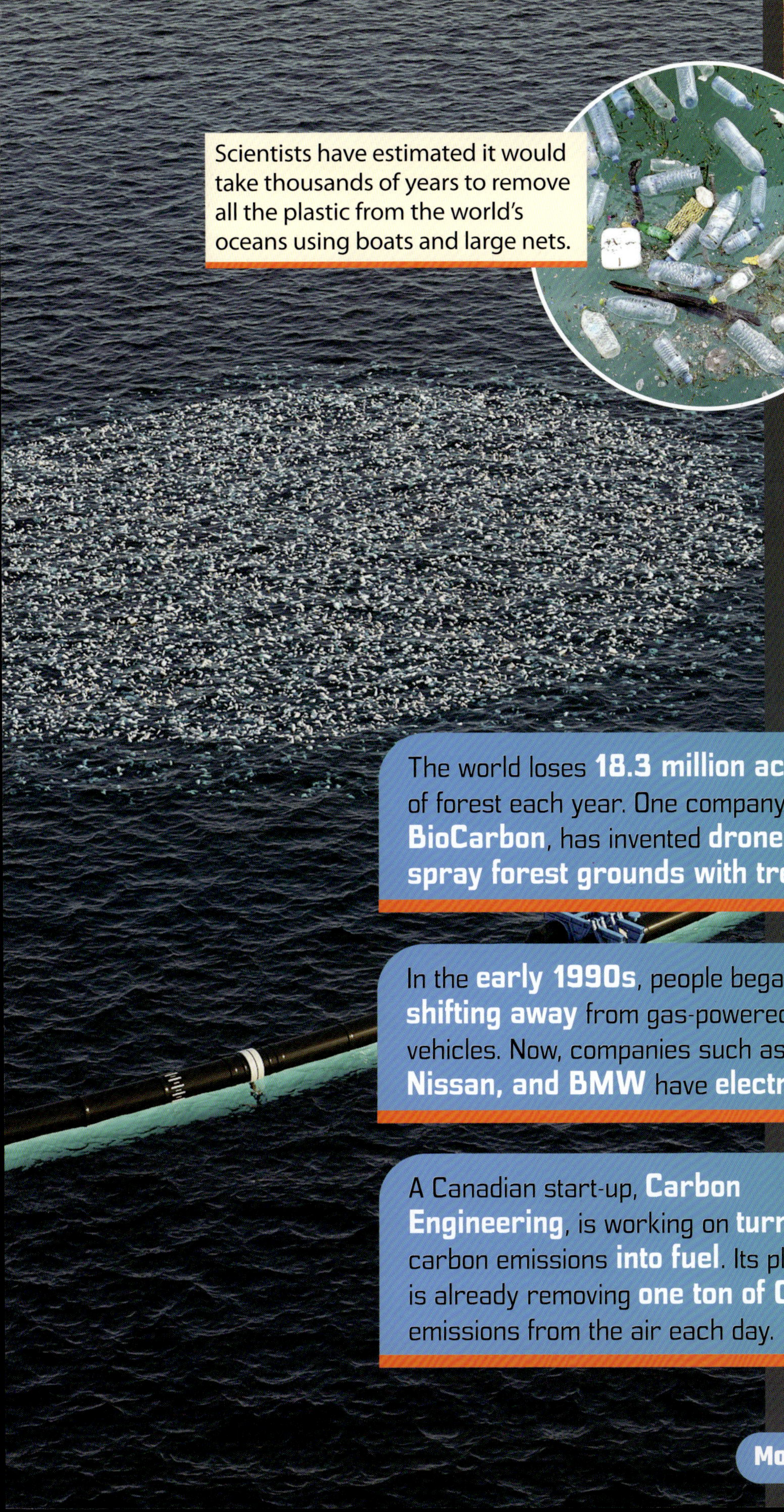

Scientists have estimated it would take thousands of years to remove all the plastic from the world's oceans using boats and large nets.

The world loses **18.3 million acres** of forest each year. One company, **BioCarbon**, has invented **drones that spray forest grounds with tree seeds**.

In the **early 1990s**, people began **shifting away** from gas-powered vehicles. Now, companies such as **Tesla, Nissan, and BMW** have **electric cars**.

A Canadian start-up, **Carbon Engineering**, is working on **turning** carbon emissions **into fuel**. Its plant is already removing **one ton of $CO_2$** emissions from the air each day.

# Ocean Cleanup: The Prototypes

In 2013, Boyan started the Ocean Cleanup **Foundation** to bring his invention to life.

Boyan and his team tested small prototypes of the Ocean Cleanup Array in tanks of water. In 2016, a 328-foot-long (100-meter-long) prototype was tested in the North Sea off the coast of the Netherlands.

The tests showed Boyan and his team that their ideas and design could be improved.

The latest version of Boyan's invention is called the Ocean Cleanup. It is a U-shaped, floating trap that is carried through the water by ocean currents, waves, and the wind. As the trap moves, plastic on the water's surface and just below is trapped in the system. The plastic is then collected by boat and taken back to land.

As of 2019, Boyan and his team are continuing to test and develop the revised Ocean Cleanup system. Cleanup systems have begun to tackle the Great Pacific Garbage Patch. On October 2, 2019, the Ocean Cleanup Foundation announced they were hoping to recycle this plastic in the near future.

In 2014, Boyan Slat became the youngest-ever winner of the United Nations' Champions of the Earth Award for Inspiration and Action.

Boyan Slat's Ocean Cleanup launched System 001 from San Francisco, California, on September 8, 2018. Its mission is to collect plastic waste in the Pacific between California and Hawai'i.

## INVENTIVE

Useful plastic that is collected from the ocean could be sold for recycling. Low-quality plastic could be burned to make electricity.

# Disappearing Coral Reefs

Australian inventor Alex Goad began work on his invention as a university design project. Alex is an enthusiastic snorkeler and scuba diver, and he has invented a way to help rebuild damaged coral reefs.

Coral reefs are home to millions of species of ocean animals and other living things. These important natural habitats can take hundreds of years to form. Around the world, however, coral reefs are being destroyed, leaving the reef's inhabitants nowhere to shelter and find food.

A number of factors damage coral reefs. Climate change has affected ocean temperatures. Vacation resorts build **artificial** beaches or boat marinas. Fishing boats drag large nets along the seabed to catch fish. Pollution, such as oil, chemicals, and sewage, harm coral reefs.

Alex's idea was to design an easy-to-build, cost-effective way to create artificial reefs. Just as we replant trees to replace lost forests, Alex believes humans should help rebuild the reef environments that we have destroyed.

Coral reefs are home to plants and seaweed, along with animals such as fish, turtles, lobsters, shrimp, and sponges.

Coral is collected and sold as souvenirs to tourists. This damages coral reefs.

## INVENTIVE

A coral colony is made up of thousands of tiny coral animals called polyps. A polyp has a hard outer skeleton that attaches to rock or the skeletons of other polyps. When polyps die, their skeletons remain, forming the rock-like structure of a coral reef.

# Designing a Coral Reef

Building artificial reefs is not a new idea. Alex wanted to create a more natural design, however, and one that was easy to build.

Many existing artificial reef ideas were large structures that required big boats and heavy lifting gear to put them in place. Alex's system was inspired by Lego. It is called the Modular Artificial Reef Structure (MARS). A diver can position the small modules on the seabed and then slot them together—just like Lego pieces.

Alex's design means a new reef can be constructed in just a few days. During testing of the MARS system, small seaweeds, sponges, shrimp, and other living things made the modules their home within a few months.

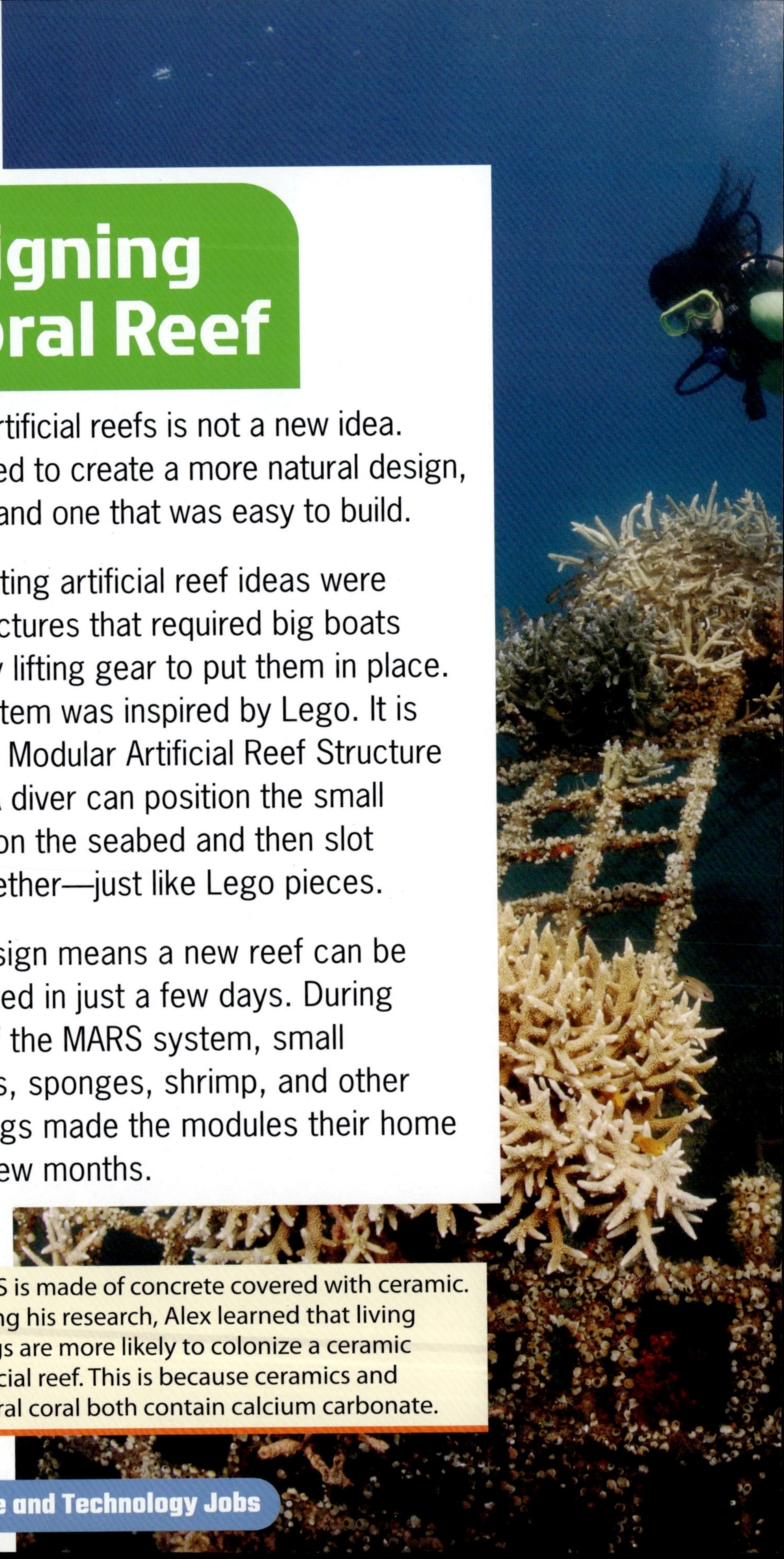

MARS is made of concrete covered with ceramic. During his research, Alex learned that living things are more likely to colonize a ceramic artificial reef. This is because ceramics and natural coral both contain calcium carbonate.

## INVENTIVE

Alex hopes to sell the MARS system to organizations that restore damaged reefs. The low-cost system could also be used by people living on small islands and in developing nations that have suffered damage to their natural coral reefs.

# Keeping It Simple and Sustainable

British inventor Emily Cummins designs simple but clever objects that help improve people's lives. She works on inventions that are environmentally friendly and **sustainable**.

Every day, millions of people, mostly women and children, spend hours fetching water for their families. Often they must walk miles to reach a river, pond, or waterhole. Then, they make the return journey loaded with heavy containers of water.

Emily designed a water carrier that can hold up to five containers and can be pulled along. Emily knew the people who most needed her invention might live in remote places with limited access to tools and materials. So, the carrier can be made from branches and other pieces of wood that are free and easy to find.

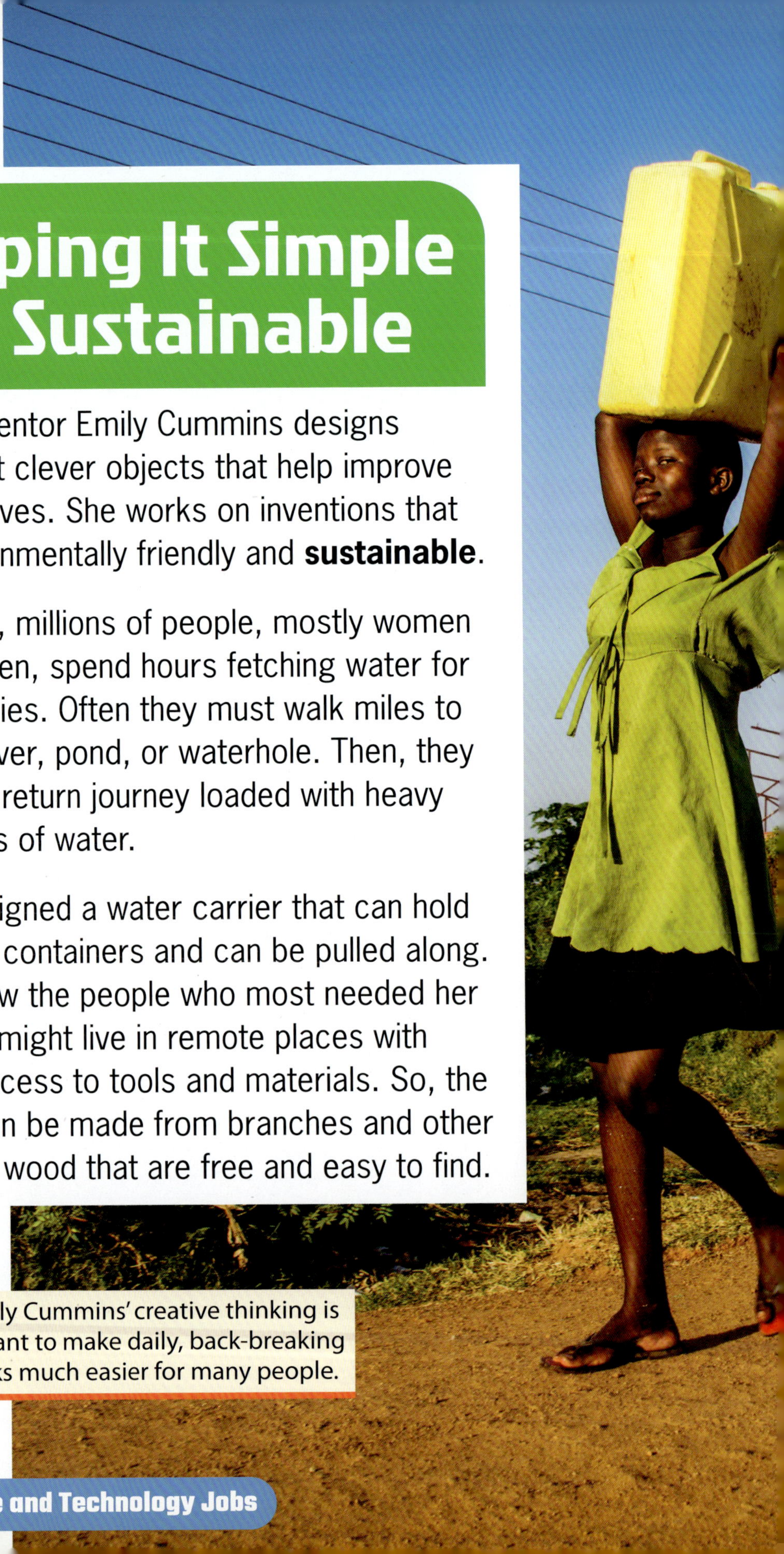

Emily Cummins' creative thinking is meant to make daily, back-breaking tasks much easier for many people.

# Water Carrier Design

## INVENTIVE

Emily began her inventing career in her grandfather's toolshed when she was just four years old. She learned how to use tools to make toys out of scraps of materials she found in the shed.

# Escape the Earth

Some inventors take **inspiration** from science fiction to develop their futuristic ideas.

In 2006, a team of engineers and designers in the United States started a company called Terrafugia. The name is taken from the Latin words for "escape the Earth." Terrafugia's goal is to design, build, and sell flying cars!

The team has designed many different concepts. One of their ideas was the four-seat TF-X. The idea was to design a vehicle that could make vertical takeoffs and landings on rooftops and in parking lots, with no need for a runway. It could fly at 200 miles per hour (322 kilometers per hour) and drive at highway speeds. By continually designing and testing new ideas, the team hopes to one day develop a flying car that will become a reality.

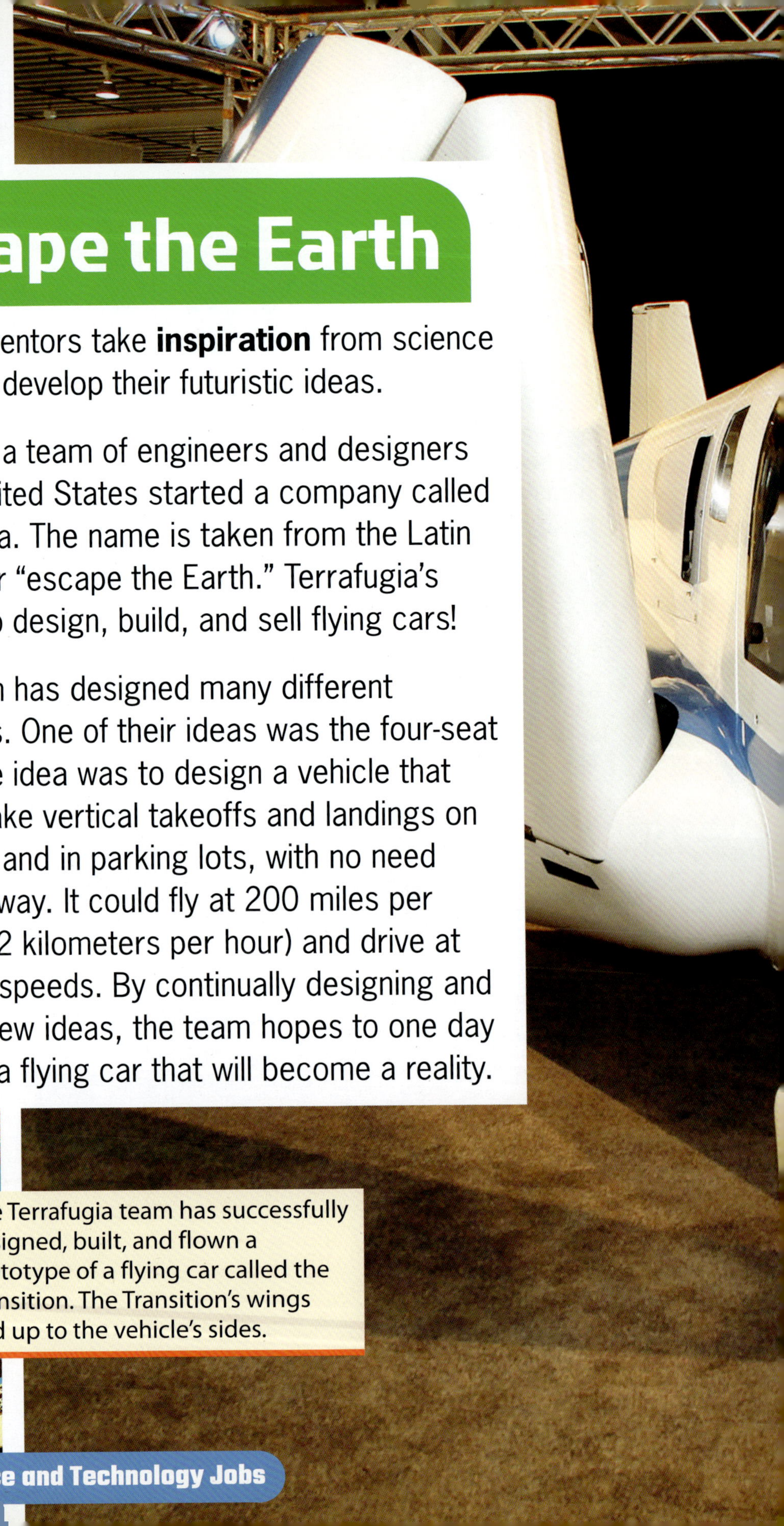

The Terrafugia team has successfully designed, built, and flown a prototype of a flying car called the Transition. The Transition's wings fold up to the vehicle's sides.

The designers gave the TF-X propellers that would allow it to take off and land like a helicopter.


## INVENTIVE

Before flying in the TF-X, a driver would program the flight plan into the vehicle's onboard computer. Then, at the press of a button, the TF-X would automatically take off, fly to its destination, and land.

# Shooting for the Stars

For centuries, inventors, scientists, and engineers have worked on telescopes and spacecraft that have allowed us to learn about space. Now we want to know if another planet like Earth exists beyond our **solar system**.

Alpha Centauri is the nearest star system to our solar system. In recent times, scientists have discovered planets in this system. However, at around 25 trillion miles (40 trillion km) from Earth, they are too far away for us to learn much about them. Even today's fastest spacecraft would take about 30,000 years to reach Alpha Centauri. So how do we get to investigate these distant worlds?

An ambitious project named Breakthrough Starshot hopes to one day send a fleet of ultra-fast **nano**-spacecraft to Alpha Centauri. Each of the tiny spacecraft will be no bigger than a credit card.

Our solar system has just one star, the Sun. The Alpha Centauri system consists of three stars.

Scientists announced the Breakthrough Starshot project at the One World Observatory in New York City on April 12, 2016.

The StarChip is an example of a nano-spacecraft.

## INVENTIVE

Breakthrough Starshot's nano-spacecraft will be blasted into orbit around Earth inside a mother ship. Once a spacecraft is released from the mother ship, light beamers on Earth will direct laser beams onto the craft's sail. Each spacecraft will be attached to a thin piece of material called a lightsail. The lasers will propel the tiny craft across space toward Alpha Centauri at ultra-fast speeds.

# Tomorrow's Nanotechnology

The nano-spacecraft will travel toward Alpha Centauri at around 134 million miles per hour (216 million km/h). Traveling at this speed, they could reach Alpha Centauri in just 20 years.

The tiny spacecraft will be fitted with cameras and scientific equipment. They will collect information and take photos and then beam them back to Earth.

For now, Breakthrough Starshot is an exciting dream. If it does get off the ground, it will be thanks to the work of inventors, scientists, and engineers.

Inventors have given us the wheel, medicine, cars, planes, computers, and the internet. Perhaps tomorrow's inventors will help give us our first glimpse of another Earth. Maybe even the first signs that we are not alone in the **universe**!

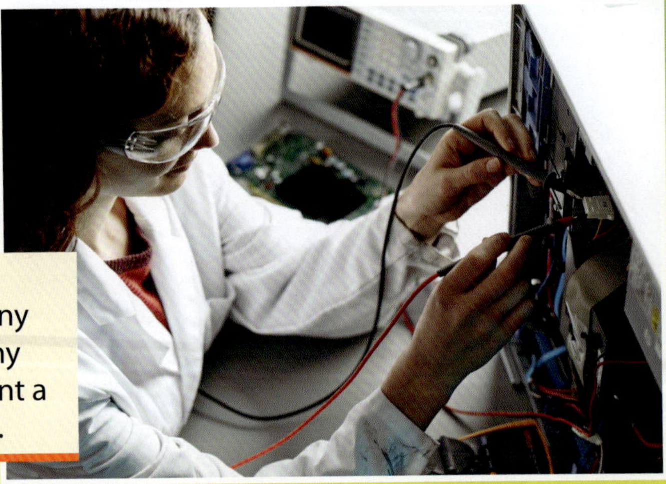

Inventors can contribute to Breakthrough Starshot in many ways. They might design a tiny part of the spacecraft or invent a device to collect information.

# History of Inventors

Humans have been inventing since the beginning of time. From a stone axe head to nano-spacecraft, inventions have come a long way.

**3500 BC** The wheel is invented.

**1450 AD** Johannes Gutenberg invents the printing press.

**1609** Galileo Galilei invents a telescope to study the stars.

**1800** Alessandro Volta discovers how to harness electricity into a battery.

**1908** Henry Ford launches the first affordable automobile for the masses.

**1969** New inventions allow astronauts Neil Armstrong and Buzz Aldrin to be the first people to walk on the Moon.

**1989** Tim Berners-Lee launches the World Wide Web.

**2007** Apple introduces the first touch screen phone, the iPhone.

**2019** The Geopress Purifier allows for any water to be filtered, cleaned, and carried in a 24-ounce (0.7-liter) bottle.

# Inventor Quiz

**01** What is the name of Boyan Slat's company?

**02** What did Terrafugia invent?

**03** Who were the first two people to walk on the Moon?

**04** What are some companies that are creating electric cars?

**05** Who invented the telephone?

**06** Who was the first African American woman to receive a patent for her invention?

**07** What is Modular Artificial Reef Structure (MARS) made out of?

**08** Where will the Breakthrough Starshot nano-spacecraft go?

**09** What calendar system is used today?

**10** How much plastic is washed into the ocean every year?

**ANSWER**

**01** Ocean Cleanup Foundation **02** A flying car **03** Neil Armstrong and Buzz Aldrin **04** Tesla, Nissan, and BMW **05** Alexander Graham Bell **06** Sarah E. Goode **07** Concrete covered with ceramics **08** Alpha Centauri **09** Gregorian **10** Up to 13 million tons (11.8 million metric tons)

# Key Words

**artificial:** made by people; not natural

**cost-effective:** producing good results without costing a lot of money

**currents:** continuous movements of ocean water from one place to another

**designer:** a person who plans and creates how something looks or works

**engineer:** a person who uses math, science, and technology to design and build machines

**feedback:** people's reactions to something

**foundation:** an organization that raises money to do helpful work for people, animals, or the environment

**gyres:** areas in the sea where ocean currents meet and rotate

**laboratories:** rooms or buildings with equipment for experiments and other scientific studies

**nano:** science, engineering, and technological work that deals with very tiny, or microscopic, things

**prototype:** the first version, or test version, of something, such as a vehicle or a machine

**solar system:** the Sun and all the objects that orbit it, such as planets, their moons, asteroids, and comets

**STEM:** science, technology, engineering, and math

**sustainable:** something that will not stop but will continue in the future

**universe:** all matter and energy that exists, including all the planets, stars, galaxies, and contents of space

# Index

# Get the best of both worlds.

AV2 bridges the gap between print and digital.

The expandable resources toolbar enables quick access to content including **videos**, **audio**, **activities**, **weblinks**, **slideshows**, **quizzes**, and **key words**.

**Animated videos** make static images come alive.

Resource icons on each page help readers to further **explore key concepts**.

Published by AV2
350 5th Avenue, 59th Floor
New York, NY 10118
Website: www.av2books.com



Library of Congress Control Number: 2019957723

ISBN 978-1-7911-2206-5 (hardcover)
ISBN 978-1-7911-2203-4 (softcover)
ISBN 978-1-7911-2204-1 (multi-user eBook)
ISBN 978-1-7911-2205-8 (single-user eBook)

Printed in Guangzhou, China
1 2 3 4 5 6 7 8 9 0 24 23 22 21 20

032020
101319

Project Coordinator: John Willis
Designer: Terry Paulhus

Every reasonable effort has been made to trace ownership and to obtain permission to reprint copyright material. The publishers would be pleased to have any errors or omissions brought to their attention so that they may be corrected in subsequent printings.

AV2 acknowledges Alamy, Getty Images, iStock, Newscom, and Shutterstock as its primary image suppliers for this title.

First published in 2017 by Ruby Tuesday Books Ltd.